The Drug Awareness Library™

Danger: ALCOHOL

Ruth Chier

The Rosen Publishing Group's
PowerKids Press™
New York

Published in 1996 by The Rosen Publishing Group, Inc.
29 East 21st Street, New York, NY 10010

First Edition

Book design: Erin McKenna

Photo credits: Cover by Michael Brandt; p. 12 by Lauren Piperno; all other photos by Maria Moreno.

Chier, Ruth.
    Danger: alcohol / Ruth Chier.
        p.   cm. — (The drug awareness library)
    Includes index.
    Summary: Introduces the nature and effects of alcohol and describes what happens when it is abused.
    ISBN 0-8239-2339-8
    1. Alcoholism—Juvenile literature. [1. Alcoholism.] [1. Title. II. Series.
    HV5066.C48 1996
    362.29'2—dc20
                                               96-14333
                                              CIP
                                              AC

Manufactured in the United States of America

Contents

SPECIAL
OFFER
30 NEW ITEMS
DISCOUNT
BEER & SODA
SUITCASE
$10.99
BUSCH
BEER
BUSCH
LIGHT
BEER

What Is Alcohol?

Alcohol is a **drug** (DRUG) that is in beer, wine, and **liquor** (LIK-er). Your parents may drink wine or beer with dinner or on holidays. You may see commercials for beer on TV, or ads for liquor on billboards.

Even though many people drink alcohol, it can be dangerous. For some people it can cause a lot of problems.

◀ You have probably seen signs like these advertising alcohol.

How Alcohol Is Made

People use fruit, vegetables, and grains to make alcohol. Alcohol is made by **fermentation** (fer-men-TAY-shun). Fermenting changes the sugars and starches in these foods into alcohol. Different kinds of alcohol are made from different kinds of food. Alcohol can be made from potatoes, apples, wheat, barley, rye, corn, or many other foods.

Alcohol is made from different kinds of food, such as corn, potatoes, and fruit. ▶

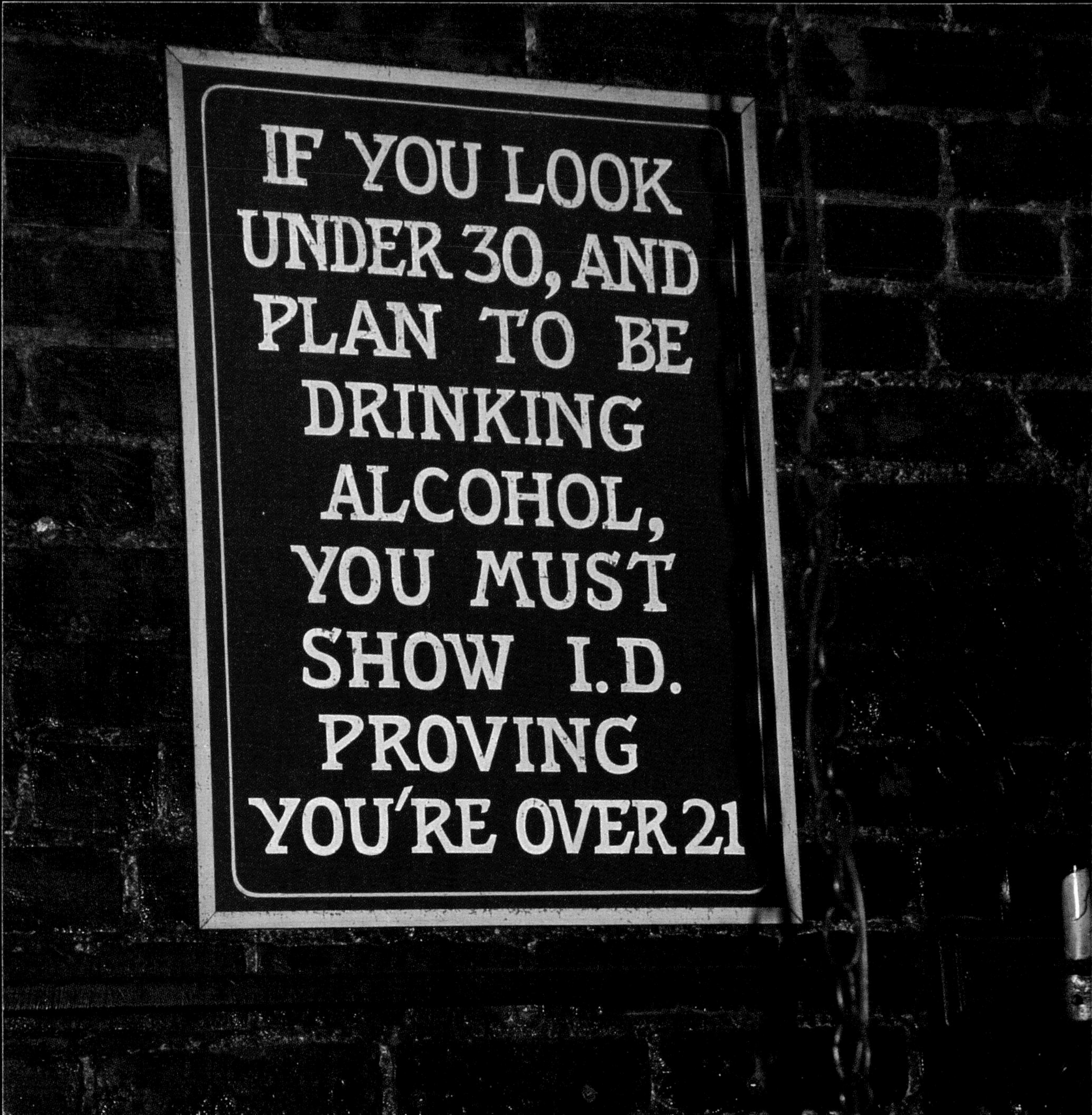
IF YOU LOOK
UNDER 30, AND
PLAN TO BE
DRINKING
ALCOHOL,
YOU MUST
SHOW I.D.
PROVING
YOU'RE OVER 21

21 or Older

Alcohol is a **legal** (LEE-gul) drug. That means that some people can buy and drink it. These people must be 21 or older. A person who drinks alcohol before he is 21 is breaking the law.

When you turn 21, you can decide if you want to drink alcohol or not. If you decide to drink alcohol, learn to drink it **responsibly** (re-SPON-si-blee). You don't want to hurt yourself or others. If you're smart, you will probably decide not to drink it at all.

◀ A person must be 21 or older to buy or drink alcohol.

Alcohol and Your Body

Your brain controls everything your body does. It tells you to walk, talk, breathe, and think. But when alcohol is in a person's body, her brain slows down and doesn't work as well as it should.

If a person's brain isn't working right, her body can't work right either. This can make a person behave differently. And that can cause trouble.

It's smart to stay away from alcohol. Alcohol makes it hard for your brain to tell your body how to walk. ▶

Acting Differently

When a person drinks alcohol, he has a hard time doing normal things. The more alcohol someone drinks, the harder it is for him to speak, drive, or walk. Alcohol also makes it hard to think clearly. Someone who is drinking alcohol might say things that don't make sense. He may be hard to understand. He may do things he wouldn't normally do. He may become **violent** (VY-o-lint) or angry. He may stumble when he walks. He may fall down stairs or trip over his own feet.

◀ When a person drinks alcohol, he has a hard time thinking about things like homework.

You Never Can Tell

No one can tell how someone is going to react to drinking alcohol. Some people seem happy and laugh a lot. Others get sad. Some people get angry or violent. They may try to start a fight or hurt someone.

There is no way to tell how someone will act when alcohol is in her body. That is one of the reasons why drinking alcohol can be dangerous. Drinking affects the user and everyone around her.

14

Drinking alcohol can make a person feel sick to her stomach. ▶

Alcohol Abuse

Drinking too much alcohol is called alcohol **abuse** (uh-BYOOS). It can make a person very sick. If a person drinks too much, it can make him so sick that he throws up. It can leave him with a headache, stomachache, and feeling very tired. Some people drink too much alcohol for many years. This wears down a person's body. Parts of a person's body stop working after a while. Baseball legend Mickey Mantle died in part because he hurt his liver by drinking too much throughout his life.

◄ Drinking too much alcohol can hurt a person's mind and body.

17

Addiction

One of the most dangerous things about alcohol is that people can become **addicted** (a-DIK-ted) to it. This means that they need to drink alcohol just to feel normal. People who are addicted to alcohol are called **alcoholics** (al-coh-HAW-liks).

Being an alcoholic can make someone forget to do homework or go to school or work. An alcoholic may forget important days like birthdays or holidays. An alcoholic loses **control** (kon-TROLL) of his life.

An alcoholic is someone who can't ▶
control her use of alcohol.

Friends and Peer Pressure

Some of your friends may try alcohol to see what it is like. They might want you to try it too. When friends try to make you do something you don't want to do, it is called **peer pressure** (PEER PREH-shur).

If this happens, the best thing to do is to be strong and say no. A real friend won't ask you again. If the pressure doesn't stop, it's okay to walk away.

◀ The best thing to do when a friend asks you to try alcohol is to say no.

21

Fun Without Alcohol

Some people think they need to drink alcohol to have fun. But you know that isn't true.

You can have a lot more fun when you don't drink alcohol. Alcohol slows your mind and your body down. Can you imagine trying to play a game of tag when you can't even run? Or telling your friends a joke when you can't speak clearly? So if you want to stay healthy and have fun, be smart. Stay away from alcohol.

Glossary

abuse (uh-BYOOS) The wrongful use of something.

addicted (a-DIK-ted) When someone needs something to feel normal.

alcoholic (al-coh-HAW-lik) Someone who is addicted to alcohol.

control (kon-TROLL) Have power over something.

drug (DRUG) Something that changes the way a person acts or thinks.

fermentation (fer-men-TAY-shun) Process of changing something into alcohol.

legal (LEE-gul) Within the law.

liquor (LIK-er) An alcoholic drink.

peer pressure (PEER PREH-shur) When people your age try to make you do something you don't want to.

responsible (re-SPON-si-bul) Doing something in a way that won't hurt you or someone else.

violent (VY-o-lint) Hurting yourself or someone else.

Index